THE CHANGING FACES OF

Cowley

Carole Newbigging
Susanne Shatford
Trevor Williams

Robert Boyd
PUBLICATIONS

Published by
Robert Boyd Publications
260 Colwell Drive
Witney, Oxfordshire OX8 7LW

First published 1994

ISBN 1 89953600 0

Printed and bound in Great Britain at The Alden Press, Oxford

Contents

Front cover illustration

'No man was allowed through the factory gates until the hooter had sounded and when it did they would come out of the gate in a solid phalanx from kerb to kerb, all with their heads down and intent on getting home as quickly as possible, a fearsome sight to me riding my box tricycle. One minute the road would be perfectly clear and peaceful and the next a solid wall of determined cyclists all trying to race one another.' (Vivian)

Acknowledgements

The authors are most grateful to the institutions, librarians, companies and individuals through whose kindness the photographs in this book were made available. In particular they wish to thank:

The Centre for Oxfordshire Studies for their advice and unfailing patience, with particular thanks to Dr Malcolm Graham and Nuala La Vertue, Oxfordshire Photographic Archives (OPA); the Cowley Local History Society; Bodleian Library; Oxford & County Newspapers; Allen Power Equipment Limited; St Christophers School; Cowley St James School; Wright/Lowe Collection; Kelly's Directories Limited; and the management of Templars Square at Cowley.

Many individuals have contributed both photographs and memories and we thank the following Hilda Bennett, Sally Brennon, Cyril Claridge, Phyllis Cooper, Mrs Cripps and David Cripps, Ernie Currill, Father Keith Hayden, Roy Hurst, Mr Leslie Hawes, Eileen Knight, John Minns, Barry Roberts, John Scott, Adrian Shatford, Janet Smart, Hugh Turner, Wendy White and Mrs Betty Williams. We also thank Adrian Shatford for his work on the maps, which, we believe, greatly assist in understanding the area.

Preface

The most difficult decision facing the compilers of this book was what to include and what to leave out! We wished to present Cowley's history in visual form, to serve as a permanent reminder of the vast changes that have taken place over the last seventy years; changes that are still taking place today with current developments on part of the old Morris Motors site.

Many people will remember 'Old Cowley', in the days before the development of the Cowley Shopping Centre during 1960/61 and, while appreciating the convenience of modernisation, still regret the massive upheaval and destruction of the historic heart of Cowley and, with it, the inevitable breakup of the community.

Cowley will also be remembered by those hundreds of people who spent many years of their working life within the industries there, either at Morris Motors or the Pressed Steel, British Leyland as it became. They too would have seen expansion within those industries and changes within the surrounding village. Mention has, of course, been made of these industries, and others, but the reader will appreciate that vast amounts have already been written about Morris' and Lord Nuffield. We have therefore treated the factory as part of the whole and not attempted to expand on its individual history.

However, in addition to a visual photographic record, we have tried to recapture the atmosphere of, what was, a rural village and have included, where possible, personal memories of the area. Two people in particular took the trouble to record their memories and impressions of Old Cowley: Edward Cordrey in his *'Sidelights on Cowley'*, and Nan Davies with *'Memories of Temple Cowley'*, her own memories of the area in the early part of this century. In addition we have occasionally drawn from the memoirs of the late Jack Vivian, former Chairman of the Cowley Local History Society. We are grateful to these individuals.

We have tried to include snippets of information about the people of Cowley; the Reverend Georgie Moore, still remembered by many people for his fiery temper and unorthodox sermons; Father Benson who founded the parish of Cowley St Mary and St John to accommodate the growing population in the area between Cowley and Oxford; Fathers Beauchamp and Whye who, together, served the parish for over thirty years; and the Cowley families like the Hursts, the Greenings, the Pethers and the Kings, who, for generations, kept the farms and market gardens of this area.

Above all, we hope that this book will bring enjoyment to many. We hope to provide happy nostalgic memories to anyone who lived or worked in Cowley or whose family members may have lived in what was once a pretty rural village.

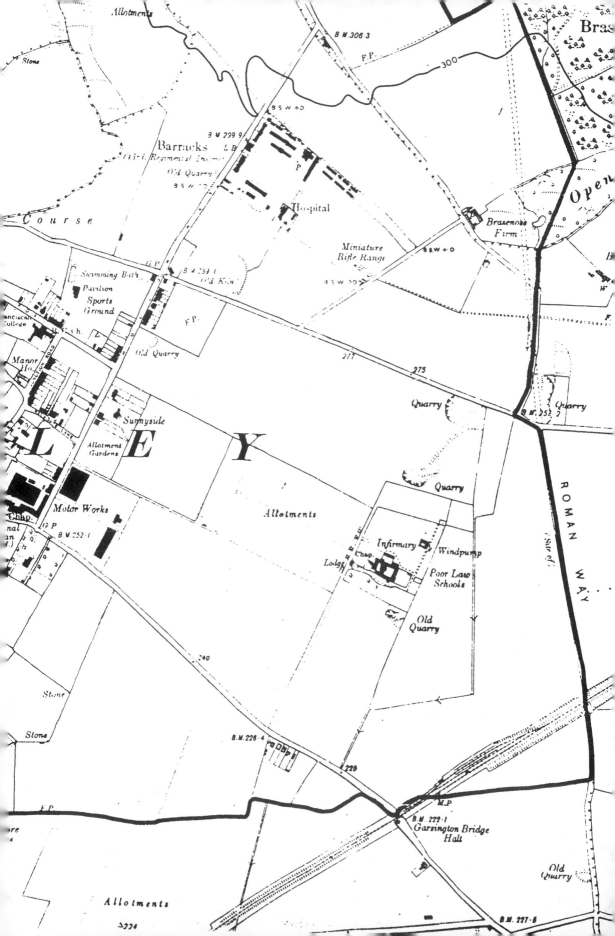

Introduction to Cowley

There is evidence of habitation in Cowley as far back as the first century A.D. The remains of Roman pottery kilns unearthed on the corner of St Lukes Road and at Rose Hill, together with the Roman Road which linked Alcester and Dorchester and served as the eastern parish boundary, indicate that there was a thriving industry here.

The Anglo-Saxon period saw the establishment of the Cowley name which originated from Curfa's Wood (Cufa probably being a local chieftain) and degenerated into 'Coo-Lea' during the Middle Ages.

By the twelfth century settlements had been established in three areas, separate but working inter-dependently. These were:

Church Cowley, centred around the Church of St James;

Middle Cowley, in the Hockmore Street area, which was originally the largest of the three hamlets, and was from a very early time under the auspices of the parish of Iffley;

Temple Cowley named after the Knights Templars who were given land in this area.

Population grew very little from medieval times to the middle part of the nineteenth century and the communities were predominantly agricultural. However, the latter part of the nineteen century saw the arrival of industry in the establishment of the Oxford Steam Plough Company in 1868. Other stimulants for change were the arrival of the railway in 1864, the Military College in 1841 and the Barracks and the occupancy of the Oxfordshire and Buckinghamshire Light Infantry in 1877.

The early twentieth century heralded an enormous growth in population as victims of the 1920s depression flooded into the community, looking for work in the car factory.

The destruction of Middle Cowley in the late 1950s has virtually destroyed all evidence of the previous Hockmore Street community which had existed undisturbed for more than one thousand years.

SECTION ONE

Church Cowley

Clustered around the parish church of St James in Beauchamp Lane, are a few remaining properties which date from the sixteenth and seventeenth centuries. They remind us of the ancient farming community which existed here for over a thousand years. The manor and rectory of Church Cowley, mentioned in the Domesday Survey as having approximately 33 tenants, passed from the Norman Lords, Roger D'Ivry and Robert D'Oilly to Oseney Abbey in 1149 and, at the dissolution of the monasteries in 1542, the property was given to Christ Church. Over the next four centuries, it was leased to a succession of tenant landlords until the latter half of this century, when individual properties were sold and developed.

'Going from Iffley, there were two ways of entering Cowley, first by footpath up Tree Lane and across the fields to Westbury and so through Cowley Churchyard; and secondly by road round Iffley Turn to New Road, now known as Church Cowley Road. The way into Cowley from Iffley was bordered by pleasant green fields, orchards and allotments, which stretched away towards East Oxford, leaving a large expanse of open country. Halfway along New Road was a rather dilapidated farmyard belonging to the then Vicar of Cowley, the Rev G Moore, and on the right Rose Hill Cemetery which was started around about 1890.' (Sidelights)

St James Church, an engraving by Buckler 1820
By permission of the Bodleian Library: MS.Top.Oxon a.66,fol 192

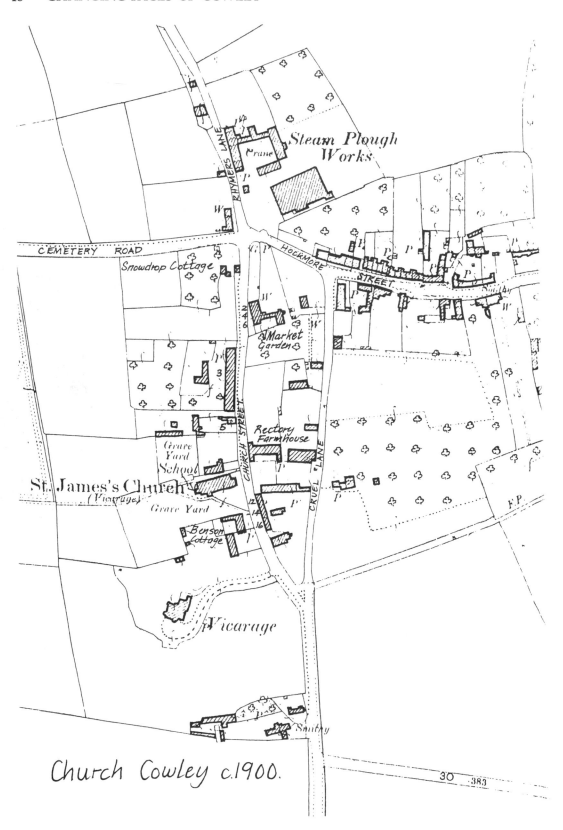

Church Cowley c.1900.

Church Street
Church Street was renamed Beauchamp Lane in 1955 after the Rev Maurice Beauchamp, Vicar of Cowley, 1928 to 1938 and Curate from 1938 to 1965. It is now a conservation area.

This view in the 1930s shows Snowdrop Cottage, now named Juniper Cottage, on the right hand corner. The thatched farmhouse, number 3 Church Street, half way up the hill, on the right, no longer exits. This was the home of the Hurst family (OPA).

Snowdrop Cottage is the only remaining thatched cottage in Church Cowley. It probably dates from the 17th century and may have been constructed, or renovated, by the Lord of the Manor to house the curate. However, the curates certainly did not live here during the first two hundred years as they lived in college. Its name has changed over the centuries but was referred to in 1820 by Rev Vowler Short as Clergymans Cottage, however, in the 1861 census it appears to have been known as Springwell Cross Cottage.

The property was sold in 1973 and was rethatched in 1974. (OPA)

' ... on the right hand corner of Church Lane was a garden I well remember. In the centre stood a thatched cottage surrounded by nut trees and in the springtime was carpeted with myriads of snowdrops' (Sidelights)

No 3 Church Street c1890. Seated in the garden at the rear of the farmhouse is William Dennis Hurst, farmer of 50 acres, and his wife, Alice Elizabeth, with their only child Bessie Lavinia. The house was built in 1596 and was demolished in 1946. The Hurst family, and their descendants, had held the lease from Christ Church College since 1768. It had fallen into disrepair over the years and was listed as being in 'a poor condition' in 1938 by the Royal Commission of Historic Monuments.

Sarah Hurst, nee Peake, of Kencot, inherited from her husband, James (1805-1850) all their lands at Church Cowley. These were to be sold and divided amongst her children after her death. In the 1851 census she is described as 'of Cowley, widow, aged 45, farmer of 50 acres'. She died in 1874, aged 69, and is buried in St James Churchyard.

St James School

In 1815 a Mrs Quartermain 'a responsible person of the Church of England' kept a school for twelve children, paid for by the Curate. The present building dates from 1834 and in 1851 is recorded as providing education for 110 children, supported by voluntary contributions. In the latter half of the nineteenth century, until 1933, it was known as the Boys National School.

The above photograph was taken in 1905 (OPA).

The School Log Book includes the Inspector's Report dated 18 December 1893 *'The floors of both school room and class room are in an unsatisfactory condition. Ventilation is not properly managed either stuffy or bitterly cold. Lighting is insufficient'.*

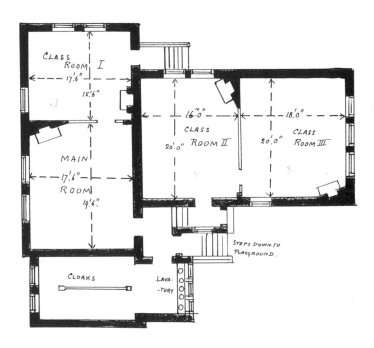

A plan of the Building in 1905. (OPA)

Girls in the playground in 1907, outside the toilet block. At this time the infant and senior girls attended school in Temple Cowley, but junior age girls joined the boys in Church Street (OPA).

1887

58

acquitted themselves creditably in this subject. *Geo. Dow-*

Rev. Blain martin — Finis —

1888

nuary 9th School reopened after Christmas holidays. Number in attendance 51 Horatio L. Turner from Carnarvon Training College commenced duties as headmaster, with monitor Leonard Kinch to assist

nuary 10th Found the books in a dreadful condition. The boys are very unruly, and have a habit of stamping their feet.

nuary 11th Had to make use of corporal punishment in several instances notably those of Carey and Peoples. The Vicar has had the maps repaired and properly hung.

nuary 12 Have been obliged to re-arrange the Time Table as I find it impossible to work to it without better help. The boys have behaved better today. Parents of barrack children — Peoples —

359

having complained because of my administering corporal punishment to the boys the Adjutant has written to the Vicar saying that he has informed them that the boys probably deserved it and that discipline must be maintained

January 13 Punished Bateman at his father's request in the presence of the Vicar for stealing coke from the coal-house. The Vicar visited the school on Monday and took the pence: he has also called every day except Wednesday. Have spent the week getting the school into working order, but am unable to give much attention to Standards I & II as my time is fully occupied with III — Admitted Alfred James Bowe this ....

January 18 Albert Capel, Fred Capel and George Trender entered school after registers were closed. The importance of punctuality impressed on the whole school. Mrs Johnson engaged by the Vicar as school cleaner

January 20 The Vicar called on Monday & Wednesday

January 24 Woodward, Pipkin & Hickman punished

The school log book records the daily life of the school. This extract of 1888 gives an indication of the records kept.

William Morris, later Lord Nuffield, attended the Boys National School between 1890 and 1893. There are several references to him in the school log book, one of which, for the 4 March 1891, is reproduced here.

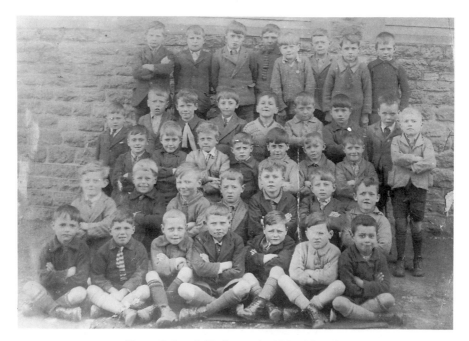

Boys School (St James) c1930 (OPA)

In 1933 the school became a primary school for children aged 5 to 11, serving the Church Cowley community. It remained until the new Church Cowley St James School opened in Bartholomew Road in 1958. St James was finally used as a primary school in 1975.

St James Church

Oseney Abbey probably rebuilt the church of St James after acquiring it in 1149. The oldest parts of the present church, the eastern part of the nave and the chancel arch, are late 12th century. This has been extended over the centuries with a short squat tower added in the 15th century and a gallery in 1820. Extensive wall paintings were discovered during the rebuilding works of the 19th century, some of which were supposed to be 13th century frescoes. Faint traces remained until a repainting of the interior in 1929.

St James' Church in 1864 (OPA)

In 1849 the church was deemed too small for the growing population (the Military College had been established in 1841) and the church wardens agreed to demolish the building and start again. However, a disagreement ensued and the parish was equally split as to how funds should be raised, by subscription or by parish rate. Those in favour of the Rate were the Vicar (David Royce) and churchwardens (J M C Bennett and James Hurst); in favour of Subscription were Mr Deane junior and Mr John Greening. The decision remained unresolved until 1864 when plans were finally drawn up by G E Street to extend the present building.

The extension to the church involved the addition of the north aisle, which widened the nave and resulted in the raising of the level of the roof, which remains higher that the tower to this day. During the renovations services were carried out in a barn in Temple Cowley.

A view of the church in 1920, clearly showing the uncomfortable position of the tower in relation to the roof. Note also the level of the path in comparison to that of 1864. The Elm trees were shading the gateway until they fell foul of the Dutch elm disease during the 1950s.

Father Richard Meux Benson

Father Benson arrived in Cowley in 1851 and was the first curate to live in the parish, taking up residence in Hockmore Street. During his ministry the rapid development of the East Oxford suburb caused accommodation problems in the small Cowley parish church. In 1859 Father Benson built a small iron church in Stockmore Street, off the Cowley Road, and the problem was finally solved by the creation of the new parish of Cowley St John in 1870, of which Father Benson became the first vicar. He founded the Society of St John the Evangelist, latterly known as the Cowley Fathers (OPA).

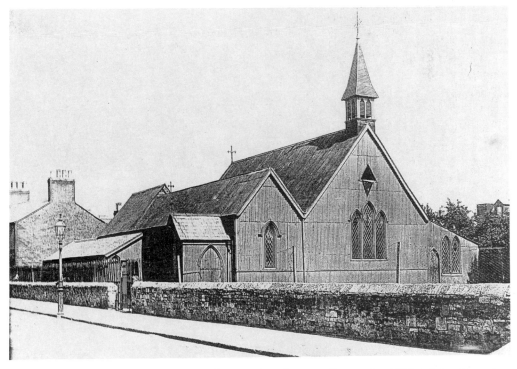

The Church of St John the Evangelist in Stockmore Street in 1896. This church was known as The Iron Church (OPA).

Benson Cottage

This cottage has stood next to the church for over two hundred years and was renamed in 1958 to commemorate the work of Father Benson. Before 1958 it was known as Church Cottage and had originally been part of the manor owned by Christ Church. It was purchased by the church in 1877 for £265 and in 1879 a new vicarage was built on the land next door.

In 1934 the thatch was replaced by tiles, the cottage was renovated and the rent raised. It was again extensively improved in 1958 when, for the first time, the curate of the parish took up residence.

To the left of Benson Cottage was a yard used by Taylors, the coal merchants, and latterly the scouts and guides have taken over the use of the buildings.

Benson Cottage (OPA)

Cowley Vicarage

This large Victorian house was built in 1879 at the top of Church Street and the Reverend George Moore was its first occupant, having resided at Manor House (Quintain) in Temple Cowley since his appointment in 1875. He lived here until his death on 24 May 1928, when Fathers Beauchamp and Whye were appointed to the Cowley living. It is believed that the Vicarage was paid for by Georgie Moore's wife, Mary.

The house was very expensive to run, as Alec Whye records in his biography of Maurice Beauchamp, quoting a letter from the Bishop '*The situation is nearly hopeless, the real trouble is the house. I had offered the living to one of the Curates in Reading, but he cannot afford the expense*'. After visiting the house on 20 August 1928 he writes that Cowley Vicarage '*was in a truly sad state, but not impossible, when decorated and electric light, gas, water and drainage put in!*' The renovations were completed by the end of the year.

The house was demolished in 1959 to make way for a modern vicarage and the Pulker Close development. '*... the old vicarage was pulled down and the new one built in its place, modern of course, but so different to the kind of genteel look that we had been used to*' (Davies)

Cowley Vicarage (OPA)

Rev George Moore: Vicar of Cowley 1875-1928

Georgie Moore inherited a parish, which was never renowned for its adherence to the christian ethic, but the five years prior to his arrival, since the resignation of Father Benson, had been particularly stormy. The situation had reached the 'all time low' when the church was empty and the school closed for a short period under the 'iron hand' of Father James Coley. The parish had seldom had good relationships with its incumbents and Georgie Moore attacked the problem with zeal and dedication, often, literally, with his fists.

When he first arrived in Cowley he lived in a house in Temple Cowley, called Quintain (Manor House), moving to the new vicarage in 1879. He was a keen farmer and farmed on the Westbury lands. He married Mrs Reid of Iffley, widow of R Reid, Esq. MP on 11 June 1879 in St Paul's London.

The Reverend was renowned for his violent temper, bad language and unorthodox sermons, one of which was based on pub signs! He was, nevertheless, a hard working, conscientious and dedicated incumbent and served the community devotedly for fifty three years.

He was Manager of the local schools and was often in dispute with the various Schoolmasters.

He took scripture classes at the schools and one ex-pupil recalls, with trepidation, him arriving in muddy boots, straight from his farm, accompanied by two large grey and white dogs. If any child moved during the lesson the dogs would attack their feet, so order prevailed!

His wife Mary died in 1901 and the Reverend Moore on 24 May 1928. Both are buried in the churchyard.

Rev. Georgie Moore (OPA)

The Smithy

The smithy stood where Pulker Close now stands, to the north of Beauchamp Lane. It consisted of two cottages and the blacksmiths shop. The smithy was worked by the Baker family, Fred and George Baker can be seen on the left and right in caps, throughout the 19th century. George was known as 'the singing blacksmith'.

The cart belonged to Silas Turner, Cowley's carrier. The tree can still be seen.

'At the top of Church Lane was the old blacksmith's shop kept by the Baker brothers. It was a great joy to see a horse shod, and watch the sparks fly during the operation. We used to bring our iron hoops over for Mr Baker to mend and he always joined them together free of charge - but in any case we never had the money to pay him!' (Sidelights)

Crowell Road

This is a view down Crowell Road, from the junction with Beauchamp Lane (then Church Street) in 1938 (OPA). Crowell Road was known as Cruel Lane and probably named after the Crowell (Crlw in 1542) family who held property there in the 15th century.

'Ephraim Hunt was a market gardener in Cruel Lane. He always wore a billycock hat, and his garden ran down to the Orchard or Lower Farm'. (Sawyer)

The barn-like building half way down the hill on the left hand side was originally part of Church Farm, worked by the Pether family from the 19th century. A Henry Pether was tenant in 1939. This view shows Church Farm buildings in use as a paper factory in the 1940s/50s; later converted into the housing development at Lewin Close.

The Reverend Maurice Beauchamp and Alec Whye

Maurice Beauchamp and Alec Whye served Cowley for more than thirty years from 1928 to 1959 and are both fondly remembered by many. They occupied the old vicarage, after its modernised. Father Beauchamp was instrumental in the building of St Francis's Church and improvements to the parish hall and the local schools.

In 1959, after more than thirty years in Cowley, Maurice Beauchamp and Alec Whye left Cowley for New Hinksey where Father Beauchamp died in 1966. He is buried in St James' churchyard.

This row of three stone cottages, numbers 10 to 14 Beauchamp Lane, are thought to date from the seventeenth century. They were built by Christ Church some time after 1620 but for whom and for what purpose is not clear. It is thought that they would have housed college employees as the workmanship was of superior quality to that usually used for labourers' housing. The cottages were sold to private ownership in the 1970s and in the 1980s were renamed Whye Cottage, Beauchamp Cottage and Rectory Cottage respectively, to commemorate the two former vicars and the Rectory Farm House. (OPA)

Rectory Farm House is one of the oldest houses in Church Cowley and the building seems to have been erected by the Napier family, the then tenants of the Lords of the Manor of Cowley (1540-1671) in about 1620. It has been the residence of various Lords of the Manor, Francis Wastie, Sheriff of Oxford 1770, John Lockhart MP for Oxford 1807-1818 and 1820-1830; Richard Hurst 1859-1870s.

In 1939 it was sold to William Organ but fell into disrepair and squatters moved in during the 1970s. Latterly it has been converted into three residences and the grounds have been used for residential development (OPA).

Numbers 2 to 6 Church Street (Beauchamp Lane) were known throughout the last century as Quartermains Cottages. During the one hundred and fifty years prior to demolition, these tiny two-bedroomed cottages housed large families of local labourers. The Johnsons lived at number 6 and cultivated a productive market garden on the land where the John Bunyan Baptist Church now stands. In 1861, Howard Ryman lived at number 2. He is recorded in church records as a *'dissenter but perhaps not irreclaimable'.*

The site was sold by Christ Church to John Allen & Sons in March 1935 and, following a compulsory purchase order, transferred to the Oxford City Council in March 1960. The cottages were demolished to make way for the multistorey car park seen below, part of the Cowley Centre development.

Rose Hill

Not everyone in the parish worshipped within the established church; there were always people who chose other forms of worship, and there were various sects and denominations within the Church of England. From 1688 dissenting meeting houses had to be registered and, in 1805, it was certified that John Bowell's house was being used by Methodists. Rose Hill, although a separate postal district, was within the parish of Cowley, and it is here that a small Methodist Chapel was founded by Henry Leake in c1835. (OPA)

Rose Hill cemetery designed by W H White 1892-94. A small stone chapel stands in the middle of the cemetery. All the material used in the construction of the new cemetery came by river in barges to Iffley, and stones, gravel and timber etc were landed opposite the lock and brought to Cowley by horse and cart.

SECTION TWO

John Allen & Sons

The original company was established in 1868 by Walter Eddison and Richard Nodding on 2.5 acres of land in Cowley, part of Lower Farm, purchased for £700 from John Deane, a farmer of Newington. *The premises comprised three cottages, two barns, stables, sheds and outbuildings, with orchard, garden and yard in the tenancy of a William Morris'.* (Allens Activities) In 1885 John Allen became a partner, becoming manager in 1887. He lived in a property called 'Wootton' in the nearby village of Iffley, moving to 'The Elms' in 1895, after the birth of his second son. In 1897 John Allen bought the business from the Eddison family for £13,000. In 1902 two houses were built adjoining the main factory gates. These were known as Cowley Villa and Enderley and were occupied by P E Greening, Works Manager at that time, and D H Sephton, Secretary, later by W Thackeray and then H E Barnes. In 1919, after demobilisation, the two sons, G W G Allen MC and Capt J J Cullimore Allen, became joint managing directors and John Allen retired in 1920. The Company expanded over the years and finally took the Allen family name. In 1973 the Allen business moved to Didcot and the Cowley site became Grove Cranes Limited. John Allen died in 1934.

Eddison & Nodding (1868)
Oxfordshire Steam Ploughing Company (1874)
Oxford Steam Plough Company Limited (1915)
John Allen & Sons (1924)
Grove Allen (1972)
Grove Cranes (1976)

John Allen OBE

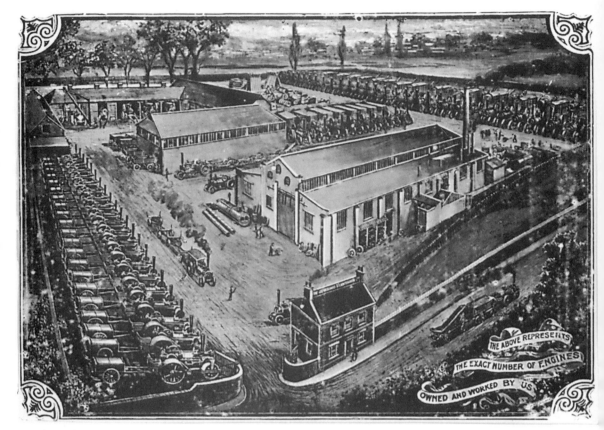

An artists impression showing the Works c1900. This is supposed to represent the exact number of rollers, threshing engines and steam plough sets owned by the company at that time. The small building in the top left hand corner is the original repair shop; in the centre is the main workshop built in 1896 but extended to many times its original size; in the foreground, by the entrance, is the original office block built 1899.

A group of employees c1906. At this time the company had about 200 employees.

The ploughing sets left the Cowley yard in March or April and worked their way from farm to farm, eventually returning to the Works for the winter overhaul about October or November. Part of the Set comprised the Living Van and water cart, seen here in the 1920s (OPA). Each Set was given a number and was in charge of a foreman, some of whom were: No 1 set Billy Maskell; No 2 Alf Middleton; No 3 Jim Druce senior; No 4 Hillsdon; No 5 Dan Pym; No 6 George Slatter; No 7 Fred Becket; No 8 Tommy Bishop; No 9 Harry Becket; No 10 W Druce; No 11 Jim Druce, junior; No 12 Dunsdon; No 13 F Clarke; No 14 Archie Garwell; No 15 Piper; No 16 Smith; No 17 Charlie Alder; No 18 Mark Prior.

The Oxfordshire Steam Plough Company benefitted from the growth of Morris Motors and the Pressed Steel Company, as a result of whose success they found much work in building and improving roads.

The demand for sand and gravel prompted the company to open its own gravel pits, Eynsham in 1922, Burcot in 1925, later at Baldon and Dorchester. On 2 April 1955 the company severed its links with the Gravel Pits, which were taken over by Amey's Aggregates Limited.

Steam engines levelling the site of the Pressed Steel Company in 1925

Photograph by Henry Taunt, the Oxfordshire photographer, of the main yard in 1908 (OPA).

A surviving Lark Traction Engine which is housed in the McAlpine Museum. Pictured right is G Harley, Chief Draughtsman, and on the left A Anderson, Managing Director c1954.

Threshing plant being sold at auction at Littlcmore c1940

Charles Richard Pulker on an Oxfordshire Steam Plough roller c1905 (OPA)

An aerial view of the Oxfordshire Steam Plough Company c1923 (OPA). The road across the middle of the photograph, bottom left to top right, is Rymers Lane. Hockmore Street can be seen running from Rymers Lane to the bottom of the →

photograph, with Church Cowley Road (Cemetery Road) leading off to Rose Hill to the left. Right across the top of the photograph is Henley Avenue, with the heavily populated area of Cowley St John across the fields, now the Florence Park Estate.

A typical gang of road menders with their Steam Roller in the 1920s.

A road gang at work on the junction of Church Street (later Beauchamp Lane) and Church Cowley Road c1940.

In 1930 the company made an agreement with the American firm of Parson & Co (Iowa) for the manufacture of trench excavators at Cowlcy, thereby transforming a country business into a modern engineering works. Excavators of various sizes were produced. Shown here is a 12/21 excavator.

Cranes also became an integral part of Allen's manufacturing capacity.

The ALLEN UNIVERSAL MOTOR SCYTHE shows its paces—

With the passing of steam power, John Allen & Sons turned their skills in other directions, one of the most successful being the Allen Scythe, a two-wheeled, self-propelled machine. The first machines were built in 1932 and were being exported by 1934. Various improved models were made and marketed, the ultimate being the Allen Universal Motor Scythe, launched in 1957 and described as *'a small tractor unit'.* This highly versatile machine, with various alternative implements, could easily and quickly be transformed for various uses. Seen here are the Spray Pump, the Grass Cutter, the Precision Hoe, the Circular Saw and Bench, and the Horticultural Plough.

Further developments resulted in the Champion Rotary Mower

The Allen Merlin, the first ever 'ride-on' mower made in the UK

Employees Christmas party 1947. Capt Cullimore Allen is assisted by his son, John Allen, and other directors of the company.

Capt Cullimore Allen had a passion for vintage cars. This photograph of c1950 shows him in a 1910 Daimler

The Fire Brigade 1952: **Left to right back row:** W Fenn, R Lee, W Spiller, P Parkinson, J Swain, J Berry. **Front row:** R Biggadike, D Wilson, W Houlton (Chief Officer) J Scott, P Osbourne.

All the local factories had volunteer fire brigades and competitions were keenly fought. J Scott and R Lee gain second place in the two man drill held at Littlemore c1952.

An aerial view of John Allen & Sons 1951.

Oxfordshire Steam Plough Company Football Team 1947. **Left to right standing:** F Sugden, J Hollier, H Belson, John Allen, P Parkinson, R Osborn, K Bailer, O Evans, D Wilson, D Kimber. **Sitting:** C Claridge, A Berry, Capt. Cullimore Allen, K Harris, K Crook.

The Dutch Gable at the entrance to the works; a well-known landmark in Cowley for many years. The works were finally closed in 1984, and the site sold for development into a shopping complex, the John Allen Centre. The famous front of the factory was preserved, but its position was changed. Brick by brick it was carefully taken down, and rebuilt a few feet back and slightly to one side.

Middle Cowley

Middle Cowley, better known as Hockmore, no longer exists. The entire area is now covered by the site of Templars Square, the Cowley shopping complex, and various multi-storey car parks. It was, however, the largest of the three early settlements.

In the 12th century a man by the name of Burgan left his lands at Cowley to the Lord of the Manor of Iffley, a village some two miles to the south-west. The hamlet of Hockmore, and its associated farms and cottages, remained in the parish of Iffley thereafter, until 25 March 1885 when a local government order decreed that it should officially be reunited with the rest of Cowley.

'Quite a number of Cowley families sent their children to Iffley School, among them being the Morriss', Paynes, Greenings, Gales, Warnocks, Lees'. (Sidelights)

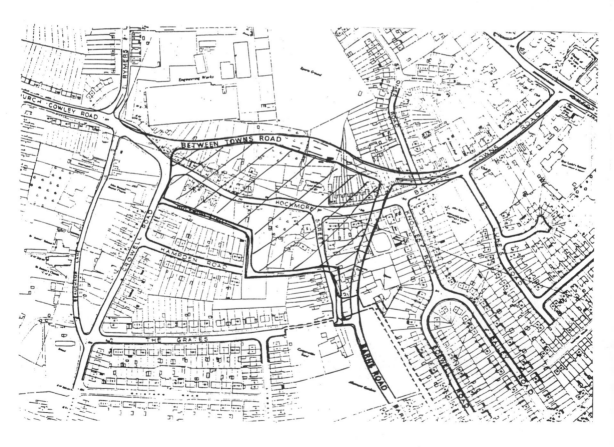

Overlay map showing the extensive changes which took place during the construction of the Cowley Shopping Centre in the early 1960s. Between Towns Road was extended and completely realigned to join up with Church Cowley Road. Hockmore Street today survives in name only, as a service road behind the Cowley Centre.

Hockmore Street

This view of 1910 shows the well known Dutch gable frontage of the Oxfordshire Steam Plough Company. The large house in the centre, which used to stand on the corner of Rymers Lane, belonged to a William Morris, father of 13 children. In 1881 he is aged 27 and stated as being a stone mason and publican of the Carpenters Arms, married to Elizabeth with four children at that time.

From the junction with Crowell Road. Numbers 60 and 58, next to the gates of the Oxfordshire Steam Plough, were substantial houses, known as Cowley Villa and Enderley, built by the company for their manager and secretary. The remaining houses shown are numbers 56 to 44 (OPA).

A similar view looking west, showing the opposite side of Hockmore Street, numbers 47 to 53 towards Crowell Road junction. The thatched Snowdrop Cottage at the bottom of Beauchamp Lane can be seen behind the raised bank (OPA).

Number 47 was occupied by the Dykes family for many years, Mrs Dykes being a well known character in the local community (OPA).

A view of c1910 in the opposite direction, eastward along Hockmore Street toward Between Towns Road, or High Street as it was then known. Number 47 is on the extreme right with Coronation Villas behind the brick wall. Numbers 29 and 27 Hockmore are the thatched cottages in the middle distance. The Carpenters Arms, out of sight, was laid back behind the tree.

An airship over Hockmore Street in 1912 caused considerable interest. Number 27 Hockmore is on the extreme right in this picture. Between Towns Road bears left at the junction (OPA).

Numbers 27 and 29 Hockmore were thatched cottages which backed onto the road; approach was made through the gardens. This view of number 27 is taken from the garden in 1958.

A view of Hockmore Street from Between Towns Road. Number 27 is seen end on in the middle distance. Number 25 Hockmore, originally a thatched cottage, was roofed in corrugated iron when this photograph was taken. Bentleys shop, number 25a, was to the left of this property. The sign of the Nelson Inn is on the extreme right (OPA).

A view taken from Bentleys shop towards Barns Court. The two thatched cottages, numbers 19 and 21 Hockmore Street, were laid back in a cul-de-sac off the road. This area was the Cowley bus terminus for many years and was known as 'The Lamp' after the Coronation Lamp.

The Coronation Lamp, at the Cowley Bus terminus, was erected in 1910 to commemorate the coronation of George V. It was a well known landmark in Cowley, but disappeared in 1960 during demolition (OPA).

Further along the cul-de-sac was number 23 Hockmore, better known as Phipps Farm. This was an extensive property with a substantial Georgian farmhouse. An Elizabethan barn formed part of the outbuildings.

A view from Barns Court towards Hockmore Street and Between Towns Road junction, showing the Nelson Public House in distance. On the left are numbers 13 to 17 Hockmore Street. Built by John Allen & Co (the Oxfordshire Steam Plough Company) for their employees, they are the only Hockmore Street properties still remaining. On the right stands Bedford House, number 4 Hockmore Street.

Number 5 Hockmore was occupied by Mr Hyde, whose wife's family had lived there for many years. On the extreme left, by the lamp post, is the entrance to the Grates, possibly so called because a man by that name owned properties in this area. The Grates was an established pathway to Church Cowley and Iffley.

A view from the Grates in 1958, showing the rear of number 5 on the left.

Numbers 1 and 3 Hockmore Street in 1958. These two cottages burnt down during demolition. On the extreme left can be seen houses built along Barns Road. At this time Barns Road had not been extended and the adjoining land was allotments.

Bedford House

Number 4 Hockmore Street, better known as Bedford House, became Cowley Community Centre after initial meetings in the Carpenters Arms. It stood where the little island is now, beside the Cowley Post Office at Templars Square. (OPA)

During 1945 Victory in Europe celebrations, Mr Albert White had the idea of starting the 'Barns Court Residents Association'. Four years later this expanded to become the Cowley Community Association which took up its headquarters in Bedford House. A new Community Centre was built in 1965.

The property belonged to the Greening family for many years and then to the Smart family until 1947, when it was sold to the Oxford City Council.

The 1881 census states that Bedford House Farm was occupied by Jane Greening, aged 65, head of household and widow of Edward Richard Greening, farming 250 acres and employing seven men and three boys.

The Nelson

Number 8, the original Nelson, built in the 1860s (OPA). This property ceased to be a beerhouse in the 1930s, George Field Gayton landlord at the time, and was left empty and became vandalised. Number 8 became a private residence when Halls Brewery built a separate building on an adjacent plot of land.

The Cowley Court of the Ancient Order of Foresters, Lodge Number 7724 'The Knight of the Temple', outside the Nelson in 1914 (OPA). The Secretary at this time was Mr A E Skinner of 126 Warwick Street, Oxford.

'... while Iffley Foresters sported a grand silken banner which it took two men to carry, Cowley had only a blue and gold flag on which we quite looked down. There used to be stalls and coconut shies, etc opposite the old "Nelson" but it never seemed to reach Iffley's standard.' (Sidelights)

The Carpenters Arms

Number 24 Hockmore Street, the centre of community activities, being a meeting place for the cricket team, the Cowley Lillywhites, and headquarters for the Cowley United and Headington Silver Band and the Ancient Order of Britons (OPA). *'... it had homely, comfortable rooms and a fine games room. At the back was a large wooden hall, avery and garden with wonderful views of Oxford. The adjoining Hall was used for numerous social events and was known as Cowley Town Hall.'* (Marriott: Oxford Pubs Past and Present)

During the 1880s this pub was kept by the William Morris who lived in the old stone house on the corner of Rymers Lane. Earlier, in 1847, the landlady was a Mrs Fanny Boulter, in 1902 Arthur King and in 1930 landlord Mr Herbert Pipkin. From 1932 to 1952 it belonged to Mrs Collier and then briefly to her daughter Olive and son-inlaw Gibbons. Finally tenanted by Jack Woodington until it was demolished in 1961.

Numbers 14 to 18 Hockmore Street on a corner next to the Carpenters Arms, in a small cul-de-sac demolished 1936 (OPA). The occupants included *'Old Jimmy who used to push a box truck into Oxford and back every Friday to collect and then sell the Oxford Times. He was about three feet high with immense feet splayed at right angles'* (Sidelights)

Rear View of the same properties (OPA).

Note the name of 'Lee' carved on the lintel of number 18, on the right hand side. William Lee jnr was resident here in 1930.

A group of Lee children in 1907, obviously in their Sunday best (OPA). Lee's orchard was behind the Carpenters Arms. **Left to right:** Edmund and Percy. **Sitting:** Doris (a neighbour), Sarah, Lizzie, Edith, Doris. William Lee, Market Gardener, father of seventeen, had a market garden on the site of the present Parish Hall in Between Towns Road.

Mr Henry John Weston and his son Arthur c1910, with potato planter (OPA). Mr Weston was a market gardener of Hockmore Street.

East side.

1 Hadland Wm. Thos
3 Tudge Thos. J
5 Gardiner Hy
7 Mapleston Miss
9 Breakspear Miss
11 Sawyer Mrs
13 Nye Philip M
15 Hine Mrs
17 Lindsey Wm. L
19 Hastings Mrs
21 Williams Harry
23 Harris Chas
25 Palmer Miss
27 Howkins Jn. Hy
29
31 Howkins Jn. E. E
33 Read Mrs
35 Webb Wltr. Jas
37 Page Ernest
39 Rose Kenneth
41 Townsend Mrs. V
43 Pegg Sydney Wm
45 Edwards Rt

47 **DARNELL A. G.**
registered   plumber,
heating & hot water
engineer.   Telephone,
Oxford 42777
49 Eltham Miss L
51 Bateman Jas. B

HILLSBOROUGH RD.

Cowley.

From 28 Fairlie road to 51
Kelburne road.   Map G 10.

East side.

2 Pattison Jn
4 Clements Mrs
6 Lewis Ewart A
8 Smith Fredk. G
10 Wills Peter Jas
12 Carter Brian E
14 Keep Fras. Jsph
16 Jones Caradog
...... here is Mayfair rd .....

West side.

Harding J. Ltd. trans-
port contrctrs
1 Harding - Saunders
Horace
3 Puddifoot Jas. Chas
5 Massey Jas. F
7 Temple Mrs
9 Miles Eric
11 Hewson Jas
13 Harvey Jn. Chas. F
15 West Alex
17 Phipps Chas. L
19 Groves Mrs

21 Pollak Bedrich
23 Eastwood Wltr
25 Fellows Wm. Thos
27 Francis Rt
29 Bennett Geo. A
31 Key Fredk. Hy
33 Brewer Mrs. M

HOCKMORE STREET.

Cowley.

Continuation of Between
Towns road to Church
Cowley road. Map H 9.

East side.

6 King Harold F
6 (rear of) Hunter H. & Co.
glazing contrctrs
Cowley Temple of Christ
Christian Spiritualist
Church

North side.

Nelson Inn
10 Hanley Jsph
12 Hinton Thos. S
14 Ford W. A. ladies' &
gents' hairdresser. Tel.
Oxford 77061
16 Poole J. tailor
20 Steele Wm. Hy
22 Parker Cecil Alex
24 Carpenters' Arms P.H
W. T. Woodington
26 Cook Ernest
28 Petch Rt. F
30 Payne Rd. T
32 Randall Mrs. P. M
34 Middleton Fredk. W
36 Hetherington Alfd. E
38 Augar Mrs. N. I
40 Lee Edmnd
42 Crook Leonard
44 Bradbury Miss
46 Williams Sidney
48 Jacobs Ronald Ernest
50 Barrett Frank
52 Biggadike Regnld. Albt
54 Hutchinson Dennis
56 Webster Fredk. A

Greening Percvl. Edwd.
(Cowley villa)
Smith Geoffrey W. (En-
derley)

ALLEN JOHN &
SONS (OXFORD)
LTD. manufacturing
engineers   (Cowley
works). T N 77155
...... here is Rymers la ......

West side.

1 Haken Godfrey D
...here is footpath leading to
The Grates...
5 Cattle Kenneth J
7 Smith Sidney
9 Blaen Jn
11 Hollier Arth
13 Slack Jn
15 Claridge Cyril Jn
17 Prowse Albt. Edwd. Chas
19 Whittaker Arth. J
21 Kirtland Arth
23 Phipps Fredk. H
25
25A,

South side.

27 Morris Percy
29 Poulton Mrs. D
39 Jenner Rd. Thos
41 Harris Arth. H
43 Cox Wm. Jas
45 Balfour Bernard Cecil
47 Southways   Transport,
haulage contrctrs
47 Dykes Mrs. E. E
49 Argent Jack V
51 Bayliss Arth
......here are Crowell rd. &
Beauchamp la ......

HOLLOW WAY.

Cowley.

From Oxford road to 1 The
Slade. Map I 8, H 9, I 9.

South-east side.

**NUFFIELD   PRESS
LTD. (THE),** printers
& publishers.   Tele-
phone 77777

1, 3 & 5 **CHURCH P.**
motor & cycle agent &
dealer.   T N   Oxford
77094
7 Poole Thos. tobccnst
9 Morgan D. (Bakers) Ltd
9 Walker Wm. A
11 Collett Roland Herbt
13 S. & S. Stationers Ltd
15 Sharp Rt. Hy
17 Voyzey Frank
19 Richardson Frank C
21 Godfrey Wm
23 City of Oxford District
Nursing   Service
(Nurses' branch home)
......here is Salegate la......
59 Way Wm. lodging ho
61 Johnson Mrs. V. shop-
keeper

Hockmore Street Residents in 1960:

Extract from Kelly's Directories, with kind permission of Kelly's Directories Limited.

Hockmore Farm and Cottages

A view of Hockmore Cottages, c1950. The cottages were sold in 1992, having been in the Cripps family for many years. The Cripps family used to have a market garden on the site of the Airfield Estate and worked on Hockmore Farm. The cottages were leased from the Donnington Hospital Trust.

The Cripps family outside Hockmore Cottages in 1917. Henry James Cripps was the first of that family to occupy the cottages. He is seen here with his wife Edith, son Henry Cripps born 1909 and daughter Minnie. Mr Cripps died in 1955 at the age of 83

Another occupant of Hockmore Cottages was Mr Henry Bowell, seen here c1890 with his grandchildren William Bowell, Ethel Shepherd and May Bowell (OPA).

Haymaking on Hockmore Farm c1915, which used to stand at the entrance to Gaisford Road (OPA). The Farm belonged to the Willmote family and was demolished c1949. Mr J Willmote, farmer, sits on top of left hand cart; Mr C Hornblow on right hand cart; **standing left to right:** Mr and Mrs Bert Lewis and their two children, Mr William Eplett with Roy the dog, and Mrs Eplett.

The Cowley Centre Development

'The first phase of the demolition work now in progress in the Cowley Centre development area will enable the new Between Towns Road to be constructed by the middle of next year. It will also clear the way for the construction of the first 14 shops, including a supermarket, on the site of the newsagents shop of C H Bentley and Sons and the thatched cottages around it. Work on this first phase also includes a service road running from south of the Bentley site to Crowell Road to the west, and a multi-storey car park to be built. The properties needed for immediate demolition are now under compulsory purchase order. Contractors have already started a certain amount of ground clearance, with some demolition, including the two thatched cottages which went up in flames last week. This is for the south service road and first 14 shops on the centre, and the car park.' (Oxford Mail)

Demolition work on Hockmore Street; number 12 just pulled down attracting local interest, and no doubt some regrets.

'The next generation of Cowley people will take the Centre for granted. They will be as much strangers to the Cowley of thatched cottages and the Carpenters Arms as we are to the Centre of the future.'

'But the first construction work will be on the new Between Towns Road, which will run from an opening above the premises of John Allen and Sons (Oxford) Limited, running north of the Nelson Inn, and connecting to the present Between Towns Road at St Omer Road. Once the new Between Towns Road is ready for traffic the bulk of the development work will start. This will take twenty four months or more. Numbers 48 to 56 Hockmore Street are shortly to be demolished to allow an opening for the new road to be made from the John Allen factory end. Premises running from the snack bar at No 54 Between Towns Road to Gibbon's Bakers at No 42 are scheduled for demolition after October. These form the corner site where St Omer Road meets the present Between Towns Road.' (Oxford Mail)

The Nelson Public House in 1958, in Hockmore Street

The Nelson Public House in 1968 in Between Towns Road (OPA).

After Hockmore Street was demolished the Nelson was left 'facing the wrong way'.

Cowley Centre in 1965, showing the extent of the new Between Towns Road.

The Nelson can be seen on the left hand side, in front of the car park.

Industry at Cowley, starting with the Oxfordshire Steam Plough Company, had gradually changed a quiet agricultural village, into a thriving, bustling, suburb. Cowley was known the world over and it followed that it should have its own 'city centre'. A photograph taken in 1965 (OPA)

Cowley Centre is losing its Bloom

'Eight years after its opening, Cowley Shopping Centre is beginning to get "the lines under the eyes" look. Arcade lights out of order, coping stones off the Pound Way enclosure, chipped mosaic on the seats by the fountain which still floods when it is working, flower tubs for long left upturned and empty - these are some of the signs that from time to time have dented the Centre's image as one of the showpieces of modern Oxford.

'The further development of the Centre is likely to begin towards the end of the year, but it will be a considerable time before the whole project is completed. It involves resiting of the 'Nelson' nearer Between Towns Road, the construction of a new Sainsbury's with car parking on the upper storeys, and the building of four more shops on what is now the Barns Road side of the Sainsburys car park.' (Cowley Chronicle July 1972)

Between Towns Road

Old picture postcard view c1907 of Between Towns Road, then known as High Street, looking north towards the Swan.

A similar view in 1958 (OPA). Note the Nuffield Press buildings, formerly the Military College, at the far end of the road.

St James Parish Hall in Between Towns Road was built on a plot of land owned by the parish and occupied by a somewhat dilapidated army hut from the First World War. The gas-lit army hut served as a meeting room for socials, whist drives, jumble sales and the like, which sorely stretched its accommodation. In 1933, the Centenary of the Oxford Movement, Father Beauchamp launched an appeal for £4,000.

After a successful appeal, and promise of a gift of £2,500 from Sir William Morris, work began November 1933. The hall was opened by Lord Nuffield on 27 September 1934. The hall occupies the site of William Lee's market garden.

During the 1940s and 1950s the hall was used as additional accommodation for pupils of St James's School.

The Old Cowley Post Office was at 17 High Street (Between Towns Road). The premises are now occupied by a firm of turf accountants. The Annual Cowley Feast was held in a field next to the post office, an area often called The Village Green.

'Cowley Feast was a major social event in the life of Cowley. The Feast was a celebration of the dedication of the Parish Church of St James and was held on the first Sunday in October in a large field opposite Gibbons Bakery in the High Street (Between Towns Road) and sometimes in a field off the New Road (Church Cowley Road) and where Florence Park now stands.' (Vivian)

Shops in Between Towns Road, numbers 2 to 14, in 1958 (OPA).

The opposite side of the road, numbers 53 to 59 and 67 to 75, in 1958 (OPA).

Oxford Co-operative

'A little past the Oxfordshire Steam Plough yard was the original Co-operative, a miniature affair of two rooms, managed by Mr Willis. Nearby there lived an old lady who used to cut our hair and gave us a lump of sugar to keep us quiet while going through the operation. I believe she was Mrs Barnes and she had a lodger, an odd character, called Johnny Rusk' (Sidelights)

This view of the Co-operative was taken in 1927 by the manager, Edwin Willis. The co-op was situated on the corner of St Omer Road, now the site of the Murco Garage. **Left to right:** G Matthews, unknown, Harry Jellyman, Arthur Sturgess (assistant manager)

In 1931 the Co-operative purchased the property next door, number 38, and extended the store to provide a butchery, shown here in 1959. Cigarettes and co-op tokens were sold from the hatch in the middle.

The interior of the Grocery Store at 40 Between Towns Road in 1959. Note the overhead cash railway which delivered payments to the central cash point. **Left to right:** Miss Margaret Phipps, Mrs Nancy McKnight, and assistant manager, Ron Piper

Co-operative Women's Guild, Cowley Branch 1926 (OPA). The first committee: Mrs Keen seated left, made the banner. **Left to right:** Mrs Cross, Mrs Barker, Mrs Bradbury, unknown, unknown, Mrs Hawtin, Mrs Clewley, **Front row:** Mrs Keen, Mrs Ansell. The Guild originally met in the old Congregational Church in Temple Cowley, before moving to a room at the Carpenters Arms.

BETWEEN TOWNS ROAD—con.
61
65
67 Williams Harold E., M.B.E
69 Jackson Bert
71 Baker Regnld
73 Evans Rt. H
75 Bentley Cecil Harry
......here is Hockmore st.....

BETWEEN TOWNS ROAD.

Cowley.
From 182 Oxford road to Hockmore street.   Map H 9.
South-east side.
2 Drake Mrs
2 Advance Laundries (A. L. (Oxford) Ltd.) (receiving office)

4 Orsborn Wltr. fried fish shop
6 **EDGINTON'S OF COWLEY,** hardware dlrs. & ironmongers, paint & wallpaper specialists, tools, electrical domestic appliances & oil heating. Tel. 77402
6A, Northfield Cecil H
8 **C. & G. (OF COWLEY) LTD.** children's outfitters, drapers, wools & nylons. Tel. 77402
10 Bollom Ltd. dyers & cleaners
12 Ownsworth Jn. shopkpr
12 Howes Terence
14 **COWLEY FURNISHERS,** house furnishers. Telephone, Oxford 78560
16 & 18 Durham A. & Son, fruitrs
20 Lainsbury Miss
22 **WHITE J. J.** plumber, gas & hot water fitter. Tel. Oxford 77210
24 Watts F. R. butcher
24A, **MORRIS & BEECHAM'S FUEL SERVICE** (G. H. J. Morris), coal merchants. Telephone, Oxford 77148
St. James' Church Hall
28
30 Cook Geo. D
30 Holton Rt. E. confctnr
32A,
32B, Hackett Mrs. C
32 Holton Rt. Donald
34 Woodward Misses
38 & 40 Oxford & District Co-operative Society Ltd
..... here is St. Omer rd ....
42 Agutter Hy. Jas. grocer
42 Gibbons Wltr. T. baker
44 Phillips Bertie
46 Bacon Ronald
48 Smith Miss M
50 Kent Harry
52 Johnson Miss A
54 Agutter Hy. J. café
58 Smith & Low, radio components. Tel. 77872
60 Goodman Hubert

60 Taylor H. J. & Sons Ltd. bldrs. (& gramophone record agency). Tel. 77044
62
64 Brooks Wltr. C
66 Bowerman Mrs
68 Baston Leonard Geo
70 Taylor Arth
72 Long Wm
74 Adams Albt. G
76 East Chas. H
78 Pocock Arth
80 Boardman Albt
82
......here is Hockmore st......
North-west side.
SWAN GARAGE (OXFORD) LTD. ROOTES GROUP STANDARD & TRIUMPH SERVICE AGENTS, motor engnrs. T N Oxford 77054
1 Butler A. & Co. Ltd. grocers
3 Bowen Jn. W. hairdrssr
17 **MORGAN G.** commission agent. Tel. Oxford 77652/3 & 78686
17A, Gardiner Harold
17A, Henry B. J. Ltd. motor car delivery agts
19 Cowley Conservative Club
... here is St. Luke's rd ...
43 Johnson Mrs. S
45 Rutter Arth
47 Bovington Mrs
47 Skilton B. greengro
49 **TYRER ALBT.** grocer & confectionery
...... here is Knolles rd ......
53 Eggleton Ltd. boot reprs
53A, Alder Jas
55 & 59 **CARAVAN & CAR SALES (OXFORD) LTD.** new & secondhand caravan agents & dlrs.; hire purchase arranged on private transactions. Tel. 77380
55 & 59 **E.P. FINANCE (OXFORD) LTD.** hire purchase financers. Tel. Oxford 78235

Between Towns Road Residents in 1960:

Extract from Kelly's Directories, with kind permission of Kelly's Directories Limited.

Church Army Press

'The Church Army was formed in 1882 and forged ahead with remarkable rapidity. The first Printing Works were opened in 1893 in Salisbury Mews, and moved a few years later to premises in Bryanston Street, near Marble Arch, London.

In 1903 the printing office was moved out to the country - *to some remarkably suitable premises at Cowley, Oxford where a printing works (the Law Stationers) had formerly been in operation. The whole property was presented to Prebendary Carlisle by Mr Winter Williams, MA (a young barrister and a great Christian worker) as an 'In Memoriam' gift from his parents. In 1932 Prebendary Carlisle was given an extension of the rent-free lease of the Works for the use of the Church Army, through the generosity of Dr and Mrs Ivy Williams of Cowley.*

For long years the Printery was surrounded by open country the building itself an old stone farmhouse where you would expect to find a dairy on the ancient flagstones inside the entrance. No wonder it was known as The Factory in the Fields.' Extracted from 'The Church Army Review' June 1962.

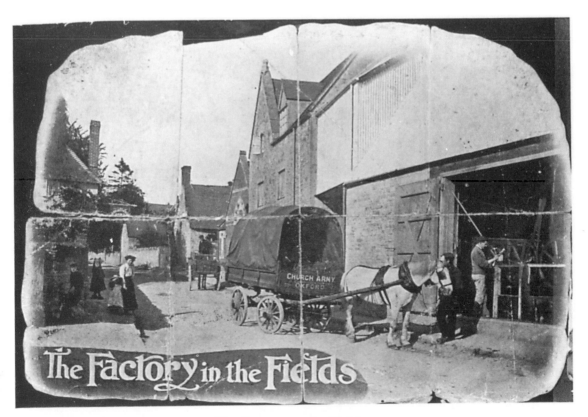

The Factory in the Fields

Main Buildings in 1930 taken from yard

Top floor: Folding room with girls engaged in folding, wire stitching pamphlets, perforating, sewing books for the binders to finish. A guillotine operator worked with the folding room to trim the pamphlets and a packer was also housed here to bale the finished products (up and down the iron fire escape). **Middle Floor**: Composing room, monotype keyboards, monotype caster machine. **Ground Floor**: Machine room. **Outbuildings**: generator room on the left, operated by a man named James Smallbone. Next comes a building that had the stereo department at the far end. Coal bunker for the generator or heating the boiler for radiators. Paper warehouse beyond. All the outbuildings were demolished when the new machine room was built and a new binding room was built.

A passageway led from the composing room to the offices, then continued into a room facing the road used as a reading room where two readers and a girl read the copy so that the readers could correct the proofs. Above the readers room was another room (with the sky light) used as a ruling department for the account books etc. that were produced in those days. The main building housed the offices, on the bottom floor was the reception office and a room for filing of records and works lockers etc. Upstairs led to the manager's office on the left and on the right the order office where the works dockets detailing the work required were written (not typed). Above the manager and order clerks offices were the binders who made the account books in leather, gold blocked etc. The building on the far right was used as a paper warehouse. (Memories of Mr L Hawes, Managing Director, 1954-88).

1930 Staff Photograph (facing page):

Front Row: (left to right): H Coulson (compositor); G Buckingham (compositor); F Upstone (press reader); Carter (apprentice); Greenaway (apprentice); Richard Kent (apprentice); ? (machine Room apprentice); Leslie Hawes (clerk); Fred Taylor (machine room); Charles Hedges (compositor):

2nd row: R Jeffs (packer); Miss Connie Ward (forewoman folding department); Miss Jessie Ball (office); Miss I Wells (managers secretary); Sid Windscheffel (order clerk); R C Kent (Secretary Manager); John Hall (order clerk); George Holthan (composing room overseer); Jo Pocock (machine room overseer); J Hopkins (stereo overseer); W Carter (binding overseer):

3rd Row: Percy Penfold; Miss Esta Chambers (folding department); Alice Bradbury (folding department); Kath Smart (reading department); Gwen Rowles (folding department); Vera Allen (folding department); Marge Hartley (folding department); Connie Walker (folding department); Phyl Thomas (folding department); Dot Hathaway (folding department); Doris Cornes (folding department); ?; Miss Vi Rowles:

4th Row: Thornton (machine room); John Dyer (machine room); Jo Ivings (machine room); David Merritt (machine room); Richard Andrews (machine room) H Shuter (reader); S Allen (machine room); Arthur Dubber (stereo department); "Banjo" Phipps (machine room); Percy Bell (composing pressman); Bill Thornton (compositor);

5th Row: Albert Allen (gazette packer); W J S (Bill) Bayliss (reader); W J (Jack) Greenaway (machine room); Bill Price (machine room); Harry Waddle (machine room); Steve Morris (white overalls) (warehouse); Harry Kirby (stereo department); H Buckingham (guillotine operator warehouse); W Laitt (machine room); Weston (binding room); Alf Bridgewater (composing); Ernie Henwood (composing); Pier Grundy (machine room):

6th Row: Arthur Chilvers (mono casket); Walter Clewley (machine room); Jim Bond (composing room); King (composing room); George Windscheffel (composing room): **group of four**: W Wallbridge (composing room); Felix Keene (guillotine operator); Ralph Hanger (gazette packer); Walter Snellgrove (composing room): **group of three top right**: Reading; R Challis (composing room); Arthur Being (monotype operator).

Rotary Machine Room

Left to Right: above machine D Merritt; P Grundy; S Allen; W Clewley with paper roll. When the Church Army Gazette ceased production the machine was disposed of and this part of the Old Barn, together with the Gazette Dispatch Room (also part of the Old Barn with a connecting door) were turned into paper warehouses.

World War I memorial to Church Army Press workers, 1914-18.

C J Atkins,   C George,
G Brown   A Johnson,
W Cox   W Merritt,
E Edginton   A Trinder,
E Eyels   H Weston.

'Sleep on old comrade take thy well earned rest. Yours is the peace of conscious duty done'

Erected by Fellow Employees 1920.

The football team of the Church Army Press, known as The Battleaxes, during 1912 (OPA). After the war the team amalgamated with the Cowley Village Team. **Left to right, back row**: unknown, Bob Kent (later became Manager), Johnny Dyer, unknown, Percy Bell, unknown. **Middle row**: Tom Buckingham third from left. **Front row**: George Buckingham, Tommy Malyon, unknown, Bill Thornton

SECTION FIVE

Temple Cowley

The smaller community of Temple Cowley, known as Little Cowley in the 13th century, grew up during the Middle Ages around the Preceptory of the Knights Templars. The land was given to the order by Queen Maud, Countess of Boulogne in 1139, and they lived here during the 12th and 13th centuries, from whence they removed to Minchery Farm at Littlemore in 1240. No relics remain of their time but their fishpond was excavated during the construction of the library in 1940 and it is believed that their chapel stood on the site of an old barn just below the Cricketers Arms. Temple Cowley was a separate manor to that of Church Cowley and when the Templars were dissolved in 1541, the crown took possession and rented the manor to Sir Francis Knollys, MP for Oxfordshire, in 1564. The Phipps family became Lords of the Manor at the beginning of the 18th century.

Temple Road originally went only as far as Salegate Lane. At this point a road came up from Marsh Road to meet Temple Road, and this was called Crofts Lane, or the Crofts, and sometime Butchers Lane (Leyden's map of 1605). This is now a continuation of Temple Road. In the 1891 census the section leading from the junction with Oxford Road to Salegate Lane is listed as Stock Street.

Temple Road 1912, formerly Crofts Lane (OPA)

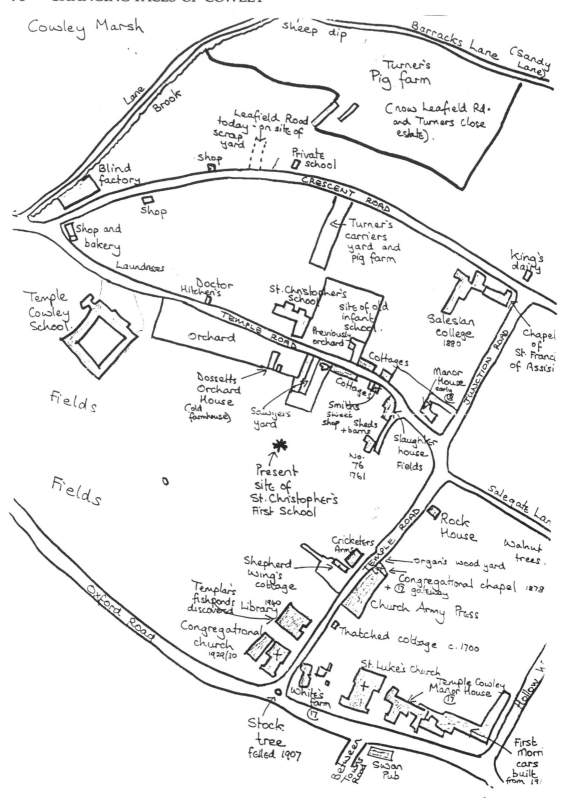

This diagrammatic map is one person's memory of Temple Cowley as it was in 1903.

The Swan

The junction of three roads: to the east Oxford Road known as Pile Road, to the west Garsington Road, known as Garsington Way, and Between Towns Road also called High Street. The Swan was so called after the public house of that name and 'The Original Swan' which still exists.

During the latter part of the 19th century there were two public houses: one 'The Swan' and the other 'The Original Swan'. A third public house, 'The Wagon and Horses', no longer exists, and the site is occupied by the present day 'Original Swan', which was built c1920.

The Wagon and Horses public house: Mr Jim White, his wife Sarah and children, Tom, Flo and Win outside c1900. Mr White also kept an adjoining butchers shop and during the 1920s had a butchers shop at 49 Oxford Road in Cowley (OPA).

The Original Swan, numbers 184 and 186 Oxford Road and the Cowley Social Club, known as the Village House, in 1967 (OPA). The junction with Between Towns Road turning to the left, looking west towards Oxford Road. The landlady of the first 'Original Swan' in 1902 was Mrs Mary Warnock.

Another view of the Cowley Social Club, looking west towards the Garsington Road (OPA). This property was, at one time, occupied by the Greening family. The building was demolished c1965, but the area has not yet been developed.

St Luke's Church

The church of St Luke in Oxford Road, immediately west of the west end of Morris Motor was designed by H S Rogers and built 1937-8. The plot of land was given by Lord Nuffield who also met the building cost of £34,000 as a gift to the people of Cowley. However, such a large donation, in addition to other recent gifts of money, was not popular with his employees who felt that he was giving away profits which should be shared with them. Feelings ran high and to avoid an industrial dispute the management introduced a profit sharing scheme at the factory. The foundation stone was laid 22 July 1937 and consecrated on St Luke's day 18 October 1938.

The design of the new church at Cowley (OPA)

The Stocks Tree

A Cowley landmark for many years, the Stocks Tree, a huge elm tree, stood at the junction of Temple Road with Oxford Road. The tree was finally cut down in 1907, but Charles Johnson, an employee at the sawmill at Littlemore, used the wood from the tree and carved sets of miniature armchairs and plates, several of which are still in existence.

Pile Road c1907 domina-ted by the Stocks Tree, looking west towards Oxford. Junction of Temple Road leading off to the right, White's Barn on the right hand side. William Hedges, master butcher, is on the right hand side, leaning against his bicycle. He lived in the slaughter house at the top of Temple Road. Mr Lamburn, a Cowley baker, can be seen in the trap (OPA).

This view of 1958 from Oxford Road towards the Swan, shows the new Congregational Church on the left, with St Lukes on the opposite side of Temple Road. The old house on the right hand side was supposedly the home of Miss Knott, school mistress at St Christophers. The Stocks Tree would have been approximately where the car is emerging from Temple Road.

White's Farm

White's Farm, a 17th century building, was situated on the corner of Temple Road next to St Luke's Church (OPA). It was occupied by the White family, yeoman farmers, for generations. James White lived in a substantial Jacobean house in Temple Cowley in 1665, which was the second largest in the village, the exact location of this property has not been established. The family played a prominent part in the life of the village.

Haymaking on Whites Farm 1901 (OPA)

This was taken on Whites fields on Holloway, opposite the Crescent Road junction. **Left to right, from the top:** unknown, James White, unknown, unknown, unknown, Henry Bowell, John Payne, Joe Buckingham (with horse), unknown, Mr Colwell (shepherd), David Harvey (carter) and Lizzie Colwell, later Jones.

This is the only remaining thatched cottage in Temple Cowley and dates from c1700. Over the last century it has changed hands frequently, from British Leyland, the Claridge family and Robert Maxwell, the well known Oxford printer and tycoon.

A small red brick and stone chapel was built in the gothic style by the Reverend David Martin and his wife in 1878. They had previously established a congregation in James Street and had built a similar church there in 1870. This building was later used by the Church Army Press, but now stands derelict. This view shows a group of children in 1892, on a days outing from the Temple Cowley branch of the Band of Hope. The little boy seated fourth from the right in the front row is Frederick George Edwin King, aged about 6 years.

The congregation outgrew the small chapel and, in the 1920s, a piece of land was purchased at the junction between Temple Road and Oxford Road and a new church, designed by G Smith and seating 400, opened in 1930. At the rear of the property was a wooden scout hut which had been built in 1928 by the Welsh miners who came, often walked, from South Wales during the depression to find work at the car factory. They could not find lodgings and erected this as a night shelter. The hall next to it served as a canteen. It was recently demolished as a fire hazard.

A christening outside the new Congregational Church, showing Whites Farm in the background (OPA).

Number 81 Temple Road, the premises of the Church Army Press in 1973. The original Congregational Chapel can be seen to the left of the buildings (OPA).

Shepherd Harry Wing is pictured above in Temple Road in 1914 (OPA). On the right can be seen the premises of the Church Army Press and behind is the Cricketers Arms. On the extreme left is the wall of the old village pound. The cottages behind the barn, standing sideways onto the road, are still standing and Shepherd Wing lived in one of them. Both Shepherd Wing and his neighbour worked for John White, the farmer.

Originally a row of three cottages, one of which was demolished in the 1930s, where Harry Wing and his wife resided. Now situated in the builders yard of J H Cox.

Cricketers Arms

The present building dates from the 1920s, replacing an earlier building of the same name. It was, no doubt, named to commemorate the prominent part that cricket played in the social life of the village. The University of Oxford first played Cambridge on the Cowley Marsh in 1827 (result unknown) and the census returns show that professional cricketers were residing in the area.

Richard Gibbons, landlord, is pictured here in 1904 outside the Cricketers Arms, with his son on a pony bought from the Reverend George Moore (OPA).

A motley group of regulars outside the Cricketers Arms in the early 1900s (OPA). Richard Gibbons, landlord, is standing on the extreme left.

A cabaret group practised at the Cricketers in 1936/37. The group was led by Arthur Whiting and called themselves the Lawrence Group. They provided entertainment at a variety of venues in the area. **Left to right:** Stella Quarterman, unknown, Marie Spencer, unknown male singer; Dorothy Bennett, ? Gibbons, unknown.

Rock House

An imposing stone residence built (according to a local resident) by W H Hurst in 1847. At this time there were three related families of farming Hursts in the village; including William Hurst 1779-1853. The house was demolished to make way for the construction of Silks Flats, now themselves empty and awaiting redevelopment. The house and garden occupied the site on the right hand corner of Salegate Lane (OPA)

Rock House in Temple Road

Salesian College

This 19th century building was first occupied by St Kenelms School, an Anglican Boarding School for forty pupils, founded 1820 by the Rev. Harry Cruickshank (OPA). In 1906 the Franciscan Friars took over the premises until 1921 when they moved to the Iffley Road. The Salesian Order educated and boarded boys from 1921. The school chapel, originally St Kenelms chapel, served the community as a Roman Catholic parish church until the 1960s when Our Lady Help of Christians was build in Holloway.

A group of Salesian boys in 1946. **Left to right back row:** Clive Bartlett, unknown, Ginger Murray, Peter Coombes, Richard Blackburn, unknown, Michael Agostini, Russ Taylor, unknown. **2nd row:** Robert Burns, David Sanger, Dino Papini, ? Pill, ? Watson, unknown, Anthony Keep, unknown, John Redman. **3rd row:** ? Simmons 2nd from left and ? Duffy 2nd from right. **front row:** unknown, Terry McAvoy, John Smith, ? Widdowson, others unknown.

St Christophers School

This school was built in 1877 for the infants of the village, at a cost of £700, given by Father Benson. It was extended in 1884 for the girls of the parish, the boys being educated in Church Cowley. In 1930 a new infant school was built and the building shown was used in its entirety as a junior and senior girls school. Temple Cowley Secondary Modern for senior children was established in 1933 as the population of Cowley expanded with the rapidly developing car industry.

St Christophers School in 1907 (OPA)

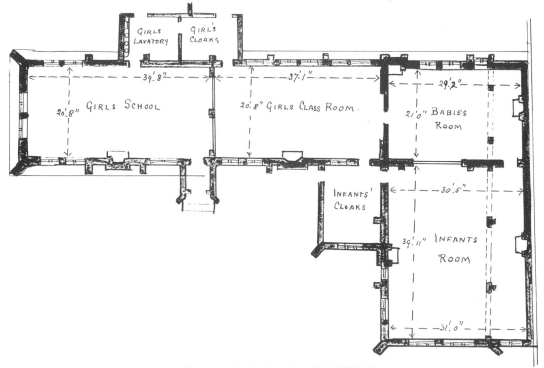

Plan of the School in 1907 (OPA)

Class A Temple Cowley Infants School, 1910 (OPA).

Left to Right standing at back: Lucy Pether, Ada King, Edna Smith, Nellie Alder, Mabel Baker and three children from the Barracks. **Boys standing:** Jim Brandish second from left; Harry Pullin fourth from right; **Sitting:** first three unknown; Bill Davies, Bill Allison holding the sheepdog Rebecca, belonging to the Rev George Moore, Elsie Davies, Sybil Thomas, Olive Aldridge, and two girls from the Barracks in Holloway.

Interior of Babies Room 1905 (OPA)

Cowley Girls School, Temple Road, c1921.

Left to right Back Row: - Bowerman, Winnie Currill, Phyllis Keys, Phoebe Pottinger, Marjorie Currill, Dolly Wallin, Mary Quartermaine, Olive Pottinger, Ida Smith, Elsie Flexton, unknown, Molly Clement. **Middle Row:** Florrie Grimshaw, Edna Clinten, Winnie Jaycock, Gladys Hornblow, Annie Payne, Ivy Sturman, Iris Couch, May Currill, Agnes Brook, Winnie Greenfield, Bertha Allison, Winnie Hilsdon, Olive Keep. **Front Row:** Edna -, Sylvia Simms, Ada Langton(?), Mabel Wilkington, Sylvia Exler(?), Phyllis Baldwin, Ethel Becket, Dorothy Lee, Rosy Cross, Freda Baldwin, Kitty Johnston, Lily Lee, Elsie Pocock.

Staff 1953: **Left to right standing:** Mrs Hickman, Mr Smith, Mr Halsey, unknown, Miss Cooper, Miss Brown, Mrs Scott, Miss Child, Mr Poirrette

Manor House, 74 Temple Road

This early 18th century building originally had a high stone wall across the front. It was previously known as the Quintain and the Reverend George Moore lived here for the first four years of his ministry, 1875-79. It is thought that the name Manor House was cut into the stone lintel after the original Temple Cowley Manor House, on Oxford Road, became a school in 1841. However, according to Kellys Trade Directory the house was known as 'Quintain' until 1906.

The Oxford English Dictionary definition of Quintain is given as 'A stout post or plank, or some object mounted on such a support set up as a mark to be tilted at with lances or poles, or thrown at with darts, as an exercise of skill for horsemen or footmen' which would indicate strong links with the military. In 1890/91 Lieutenant Col Arthur Macartheney lived here, principle of the Military College.

No 76 Temple Road was home of the Hedges family at the turn of the century. They were butchers and had a shop in the covered market in Oxford, which still exists today. At the rear of this property was a slaughter house 'a small building not much bigger than a shed' according to a local resident. *'... on cattle market days the cattle were brought by the butchers, so nearly every Wednesday we would have to run indoors, because some cattle would be driven, usually by two men, all through the town to Hedges Slaughter House'. (Davies)*   On the right can be seen the railings outside Quintain and on the left a lane, now a private section of Temple Road, but formerly known as Springview.

Further down the private lane is No 78 Temple Road, another imposing stone house, with a date stone in the gable, WH 1761. A branch of the Hurst family possibly lived here during the early part of this century.

Crescent Road

The Cowley Bakery Stores were kept by Mrs Honor, pictured outside her door in 1895, with daughter Daisy. Daisy, baptised Sarah Rebekah Daisy in 1885, was the eldest child of Harry and Eliza Honour. There was a younger daughter Alice Jane. This building, at the junction of Temple Road on the right and Crescent Road on the left is still a general store.

Crescent Road was a muddy track, with deep ruts, as can be seen in this view of 1906 (OPA).

Cowley Marsh and Area

The Cowley Marsh was a wet low-lying open space, bordered by stately elms, stretching from Marsh Road to St Bartholomew's Chapel, and from Cricket Road to Barracks Lane, formerly Cowley Marsh Footway, also referred to, for obvious reasons, as Mud Lane. During the 19th century the Marsh was well used for cricket matches, both by the University and Cowley's own talented sportsmen. *'Cowley could boast of one of the best of the new style of bowlers, followers of Lillywhite, in the person of David Burrin, whose skill was often the theme of conversation on the marsh. The Bacon family, strict devotees to the willow, were then all inhabitants of Cowley; these, with four of the Hurst, and two of the Hodgkins families, gave a great impetus to the game'. Cowley Cricket c1850.* Indeed, many Cowley inhabitents were associated with cricket; as players, cricket bat or ball makers, or groundkeeper. The University Golf Course was at Cowley Marsh from 1875 until 1923, when it moved to Southfield.

Henry Taunt's beautiful study of children playing in the sheep dip along Barracks Lane. July 1914 (OPA). Taunt tells us of two boundary stones, which had disappeared by 1914, *'... but there is a third by the sheep washing place which records the beating of the bounds in 1892, when T W Ansell was Mayor and W S Carver, Sheriff.'*

Barracks Lane

Barracks Lane, from a spot just to the east of Bartlemas, to the north of Temple Cowley, joins the present day Holloway, formerly Barracks Road, at Turners Close. Part of Barracks Lane, that running along the east part of Cowley Marsh, used to be known as Lovers Walk. Further along the Lane, to the east and towards Holloway, stood the ruins of Bullingdon Castle. This strange building, believed to be on the site of the former Bullingdon sheep-pen, is a folly with castellated walls, hence the name Castle. A family by the name of Windows lived here in the latter part of the nineteenth century (OPA).

A view of 1900 from Southfield Golf Course towards Crescent Road. The Salesian College can be seen at the top of the hill and St Christophers School to the right (OPA).

Cowley Road towards Oxford 1920s. Note the house on the left: Rivera was the home of Henry Taunt, the Oxfordshire photographer, who had a shop in Broad Street and also a workshop behind his home. This property is now part of the City of Oxford Bus Station.

Southfield Farm, Cowley Road c1914, now the site of Oxford Boys School, formerly known as Southfield School.

Cowley Road, from Oxford to Temple Road, was formerly known as Berry Lane (1605 Christ Church map) and crossed the Marsh as a causeway, changing its name to Pile Road, now Oxford Road, in the process.

Pile Road, towards Cowley from the Marsh, from an old postcard view of c1910 (OPA).

Oxford Road c1912, looking west towards Oxford (OPA). The houses on the left remain virtually the same.

St Bartholomews

St Bartholomews, known from very early times as the Bartlemas, is visually screened from the busy Cowley Road and stands on the line of what was once the old drove road from Oxford over Shotover to London. The Hospital with its Chapel was founded by Henry I in 1126, three years after the founding of St Bartholomews Hospital in London. It was intended as a hospital for lepers; hence its position well outside the city wall. In 1329 Edward III transferred the hospital revenues to Oriel College, landlords to this day. By the 16th century leprosy was disappearing in Europe and the Bartlemas evolved into an almshouse and refuge from the Plague, also a convalescent home following the cholera epidemics of the 19th century. During the civil war the Hospital was raised to the ground; the Chapel survived although the lead was stolen from the roof and the chapel bells disappeared. The Hospital was rebuilt by Oriel in 1649.

In 1900 Bartlemas was brought within the boundaries of the newly formed parish of Cowley St John, the parish church of which, SS Mary and John, was built in 1875, not far from Bartlemas. The Chapel has again been in continuous occasional use since 1913; from 1941 to 1949 as a place of worship for the Russian Orthodox congregation.

In the early 1980s the hospital buildings, now called Bartlemas House, along with Bartlemas Farmhouse and Bartlemas Cottage, were sold to various private owners who have undertaken the day to day care of Bartlemas.

Bartlemas from the south-west in 1908 (OPA).

St Bartholomew's Chapel

Bartlemas House

Hollow Way

'At the junction of Temple Cowley Street and the Garsington way was the Hollow Way. This was really "hollow" and lay between steep, high banks surmounted by lofty elm trees, and was probably the road down which the timber and stone for building purposes were hauled from Shotover Forest and various quarries. At its other end Hollow Way opened out widely into Bullingdon Green. In 1849 when the Enclosure Act was passed, many changes were effected by the Commissioners: the surface of Hollow Way was considerably raised and the road continued across Bullingdon Green to the Slade; part of Salegate Lane was closed, and the remainder joined to Hollow Way'
(White)

The Barracks, home of the Oxfordshire and Buckinghamshire Light Infantry until 1959, was built in 1877 on Bullingdon Green. *'It was one of the highlights of the week for the youngsters to gather and watch the Red Coats swing past to parade to Church Lane before marching into Church' (Vivian).* Military graves can be seen in the southwest of St James churchyard and the Church holds several brass plaques with the names of two hundred members of the Regiment and their families who died while on military service - many of them from disease. The Barracks children attended the local schools, and the Rev Georgie Moore was chaplain.

To the south of the Barracks is the catholic church Our Lady Help of Christians, built in 1961 and to the north is St Francis, originally a temporary church hall built in 1930, on a site given by Morris Motors.

In 1921 a house and grounds in Hollow Way was given to the Radcliffe Infirmary by Dr Ivy Williams, and in 1922 it was opened as Sunnyside Convalescent Home for women and children. In 1930 the Cowley property was sold and the home moved to the Headington Manor site.

In 1929 the Bullingdon Estate, at the far end of Hollow Way, was developed near to the Slade, originally site of a war training camp the buildings of which were used as a prisoner of war camp. Prisoners were often to be seen working on local farms.

A postcard view from the junction of Hollow Way with Oxford Road, the Military College on the left. A continuation of Hollow Way, Surman's Lane, used to continue across the Oxford Road towards Church Cowley. This led across the fields on which the Convent and the estate west of it now stands. It joined Church Path, now known as the Grates, and so to the Church.

The parade of shops in Hollow Way. Church's, motor and cycle agent and dealer, was particularly well known.

Fernhill Road to the east of Hollow Way is part of the Sunnyside Estate laid out during the 1930s to accommodate the growing workforce at Morris Motors. This photograph commemorates a street party held to celebrate Coronation Day 1953.

Cowley Football Club, 'the Lillywhites', in 1922: winners of the Oxfordshire Senior Cup. This photograph was taken on the Club's football ground in Hollow Way (OPA). **Left to right, standing:** C H Bevercombe (Sec.), P J Wyett, L Battersby, G Buckingham, E Bowerman. **Middle row:** W Bennett, J King, Guy Sturges, E M Martin, L Rogers. **Front row:** George Sturges, G Bennett.

The Barracks

Further north along Hollow Way, towards the Slade, stands the remaining buildings of the Barracks, home to the Oxfordshire and Buckinghamshire Light Infantry. Both Regiments were first raised in the mid 1700s, the 43rd becoming the Monmouthshire Regiments and the 52nd becoming the Oxfordshire Regiment in 1782. In 1881 the 43rd united with the 52nd to become the Oxfordshire Light Infantry, becoming known as the Oxfordshire and Buckinghamshire Light Infantry from 1908.

The Regimental Depot moved from Cowley Barracks to Winchester in 1958 but a small Regimental Headquarters was established in part of the Barracks, since moving to the Slade. On 1 January 1966 the regiments became the Royal Green Jackets.

The Keep and Entrance, Hollow Way 1907 (OPA)

A view from the Quad c1890 (OPA)

The Men's Quarters at Cowley Barracks from a Taunt postcard.

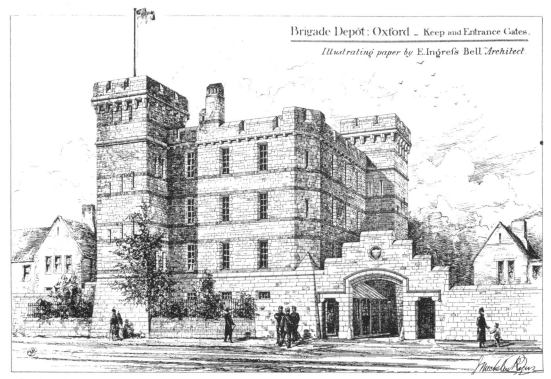

The Keep and Entrance Gates from an illustrated paper of c1890 by E Ingress Bell, Architect (OPA)

Alongside the eastern by-pass, opposite Horspath Driftway, lies Brasenose Farm, now surrounded by industrial estates and busy roads. This idyllic view of 1916 shows different surroundings (OPA).

Cowley Industrial School

The Poor Law (Mixed) School was built in 1854, by the Oxford Guardians of the Poor, and was called the Cowley Industrial School. It was situated in the middle of open fields, the nearest building being one and a half miles away. It remained isolated until industrial growth in Cowley escalated in the 1920s. It catered for orphans, children, those deserted by their parents or for children whose parents were in the Workhouse. The children were segregated into three classes; infants and children under seven, girls over seven, and boys over seven. During classes and meal times communication was forbidden. They received eighteen hours instruction a week in reading, writing, arithmetic and religion as well as training in agriculture, industry or housework. Regulation clothes were issued and all school activities, including meal times, were controlled by the sound of the school bell. Children were allowed to stay at the school until they were sixteen years of age when they were found employment. If no employment was found they were sent to the Workhouse, although this was a rare occurrence. Conditions were very hard, but the children's welfare was looked after by a Board of Guardians, who made regular visits and who had the ultimate responsibility for the school.

The School became known as 'The Poplars' about 1920, named after seven poplar trees which stood in the grounds behind the School. At the outbreak of the Second World War the School was closed, and the children sent to other parts of the City. The buildings were incorporated into the Pressed Steel Factory, but over the years became dilapidated and, with the exception of the small hospital block which still stands, were finally demolished in 1988.

The front of the school c1915

This postcard view, date stamped 1916, illustrates the complete rural isolation of the school, surrounded as it was by fields in all directions (OPA). The school was basically self sufficient; growing its own vegetables and keeping pigs and chickens in the yards. The card reads *'How do you like this? It is our school. The lamb you see is now dead. The field it is in belongs to the school, and the gardens are at the back. Thanks for invitation'.*

A view of the Poplars during construction of the Pressed Steel site c1925.

A group of children c1915: **Back Row:** Jack Carter, Jim Carter, Ronnie Beale, Percy Broad, Reggie Broad, Charlie Brooks, Freddie Clarke. **Second Row:** Connie Austin, Carrie Philips, Nora Bentley, Ivy Cox, Jack Bedding, Willie Clarke. **Front Row:** Ernest Bowden, Dolly Cox, George Carter, Ethel Bloxham, Billie Cadle, Gladys Cox, Sidney Clifton, Verona Buckle, Kenneth Amos.

Dancing was a school activity in the 1920s and 1930s. Here we see a Country Dance Team which represented the school in competitions c1920.

A School Reunion took place every year at Whitsun. This photograph of old pupils and staff in 1938 was taken outside the School Chapel.

A War Memorial Board used to hang in the School Chapel, but disappeared during the demolition of the main buildings, being rediscovered a few years ago.

John T Bushnell	HMS Vanguard
James Michaux	HMS Indefatigable
Arthur Walker	HMS Hampshire
Frederick Ballard	Sergt Royal Berkshire Rt.
Charles Clarke	Royal Buffs Rt
Arthur Clifford	Oxford & Bucks LI
George Devine	Loyal North Lancs Rt
James Green	Oxford & Bucks LI
Frederick Hutt	Oxford & Bucks LI
Alfred Jackson	Oxford & Bucks LI
James Jones	Somerset LI
George Lake	Oxford & Bucks LI
Francis Lowe	Cameron Highland LI
James Morris (Mould)	Sergt Highland LI
Gilbert Ridge	Royal Welsh Fusiliers
Thomas Smith	Royal Buffs Rt
Ernest Warrick	Worcestershire Rt
Percy Williams	Sergt Canadian Contingent

and other unrecorded members of this school who in the Great War 1914-1919 laid down their lives on behalf of King and country and faith and freedom.
'True love by death, true love by life is tried. Live thou for England: we for England died.'

Manor to Military

The original Manor House building, with its two gabled front, dates from the 17th century and was enlarged in the 18th century. It ceased to be a private residence in 1841 when it became Cowley College, later known as Hurst's Grammar School. *'The school was established in 1841 by Oxford Diocesan Board of Education for the purpose of providing the middle classes with first class education at as low a cost as possible'* (Kelly's Directory).

Frederick Morris, the father of William Morris, later to become Lord Nuffield, attended this school in his youth and was senior boy. The Art Master at the College, J V Richardson, made a drawing between 1848 and 1856 which is almost identical to the photograph below, taken in 1905; the only substantial difference being the growth of vegetation on the stonework.

Temple Cowley Manor House 1905 (OPA)

In 1852 the building was extended and the L-shaped school room erected on the corner of Oxford Road and Hollow Way.

The School Chapel was added in 1870, designed by Edward George Bruton of Ship Street Oxford. It bridged the gap between the Manor House and the Schoolroom. Thirteen years later a wooden organ loft was built and two stained glass windows installed, but by this time the school had closed. During 1914 the Chapel served the community as a local place of worship. The school's first headmaster was J M C Bennett, who died in 1868. There is a memorial brass plate to his memory in St James's church. His successor, Robert Hurman, was less successful, as in 1876 the buildings of what was now known as Hurst's Grammar School were for sale.

Oxford Military College

When the site was purchased in July 1876 the buildings were in a poor state, the accommodation cramped and the price inflated. The college opened on 6 September with six students and there were 141 present by 1881. The role of the school was twofold in that it prepared boys for military service but also provided the equivalent of a public school preparation for university.

In 1877 Thomas Graham Jackson, architect designed the East Wing and the foundation stone for this was laid 21 July 1877 by the Earl of Morley. The college was finally declared bankrupt in 1896. Some years later T G Jackson stated *'.. the military college at Cowley which, by the way, never prospered, being neither civil nor military, under a governor who did not teach and a headmaster who had no authority, it languished and expired'.*

The Military College, viewed from the south.
This market garden is now the site of Our Ladies School and Convent

A celebration of the visit of the Duke of Cambridge c1890. This quad is now part of Nuffield Press (OPA).

The first industrial use of the site was in 1899 by Alfred Breese Limited, a London firm of mechanical engineers and manufacturers. They made 'Bee' braces and 'North Road Cycles' and was known as the Manor Works. He reinstalled the Manor House as a residence and lived there until 1905, when the premises were put up for sale.

In 1912 William Morris purchased the site and Morris Cars began to be produced in Cowley and Morris occupied the Manor House for a period. The building eventually became structurally unsound and was finally demolished in 1957.

Military to Motor

William Richard Morris was born in Worcester in 1877. He came to Oxford at an early age and as a boy he played on the fields which were later to be covered by Morris Motors Limited.

At the age of 16 he set himself up as a cycle manufacturer and repairer. From bicycles he progressed to motor cycles and finally realised his dream of producing a cheap, reliable motor-car. It was not until 1913, however, that he sold his first Morris Oxford. This first model 'The Morris-Oxford Light-Car', was a two-seater with a 8.9h.p. engine, priced at £165.

Progress was halted during the first World War when the factory was used for munitions manufacture. It was during this period that methods of flow line assembly were first introduced. By 1924 Morris was exporting and in 1925 he established his own Press, Morris Oxford Press, which became the Nuffield Press in 1942.

Car production ceased again during the second World War and the Cowley factory was turned over to munitions, and here was established the headquarters of the Civilian Repair Organisation and No.1 Repair Depot and during the war years thousands of damaged aircraft were repaired at Cowley.

His services to industry were recognised by the conferment of a barony in 1934, and in 1938 the first Baron Nuffield was created a viscount.

William Richard Morris, The Viscount Nuffield.
Born 10 October 1877, died 22 August 1963.

William Morris bought the redundant Military College in 1912 to expand his motor car manufacture. The East Wing, facing Hollow Way, was converted for the purpose. Parts were received on the ground floor, chassis frames were assembled on the first floor and the engines and wheels fitted. The car bodies were fitted to the chassis on the second floor and the loft was used for storing and painting wheels.

In 1914 Morris erected a one-storey steel framed building over part of the Military College parade ground for a new assembly area, generally known as the Old Tin Shed, and expansion had started.

Morris Motors from the market garden belonging to the Smart family
looking across Hollow Way c1914 (OPA).

Production 1925

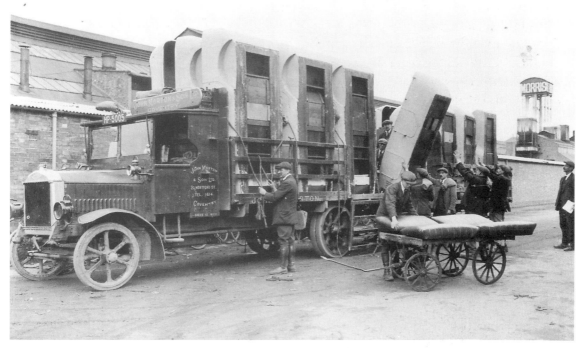

Car bodies arriving from the Coventry Works.

Final test run in the Garsington Road.

Production 1935

Body Assembly

Final View

A group of women munition workers at Morris Motors during the First World War (OPA).

A rail track ran from Hollow Way along the Garsington Road to Cowley Railway Station, carrying munitions day and night.

During the Second World War No 1 Civilian Repair Unit at Cowley was the largest of its type, where damaged aircraft were taken for repair or salvage of parts. The whole operation was headed by Lord Nuffield. The car despatch department, on the south side of Garsington Road, became a giant hanger and workshop and car mechanics became aircraft mechanics. Cowley became known as 'The Outpatients Department' where aircraft were patched up and returned to active duty as quickly as possible. Parts of alloy, rubber and plastic were extracted from those aircraft beyond repair and accumulated at No 1 MPRD (Metal Produce and Recovery Depot) along the Garsington Road.

Morris Motor rooftops, towards Oxford. Despite the rapid expansion of the factory, and the impact it must of had upon surroundings and the local population, Cowley was still very much a village.

An aerial view of the factory complex, c1936. The original Military College, with St Lukes Church, is at the bottom right hand side of the picture, looking east towards Garsington. The large oval which can be seen near the top right hand side, near the line of trees, is the Oxford Greyhound Stadium.

The expansion of the industry drew thousands of people looking for employment to the Oxford area. They came from all parts of the British Isles. Soon housing estates were springing up around the factory to cater for the influx of labour and a quiet village was rapidly disappearing.

A typical scene at the end of the day, with the workforce making a hasty dash for home.

A depressing scene, but one very familiar to those who lived in such close proximity to the factory. This part of the factory, the paint shop, has now been demolished and is currently under development.

The Birth of the Pressed Steel Company 1926.
William Morris became interested in the all-steel chassis and Morris Motors Limited helped to finance the setting up of the Pressed Steel Company on land adjacent to the motor works.

During construction of the eastern by-pass, showing the expansion of the Pressed Steel factory. 'The Poplars' Chapel can be seen facing the new by-pass.

A view taken from the main office block of Pressed Steel, looking north. 'The Poplars' can be seen hiding behind the engineering block. The seven poplar trees gave the building its name. Interdepartmental sporting competitions were an extremely popular part of factory life.

Chassis Department XI
Winners of the Inter Dept Football Cup 1929/30

Left to right back row: D Hathaway (F.C Representative), L B Didcock, W Middleton, L Miller, W A Porter, S L Claridge (F.C Hon Sec.). **Middle row:** J Drake, D Hunt, C V Harris (Captain), F W Woodley, F W Wise. **Front row:** A Ryan, W N Morgan

Development of the Rover Site

The car assembly plant was closed in December 1992 and demolition work commenced in February 1993. The first phase of development commenced in October 1993. As part of the initial phase a multi-lane flyover was constructed to ease the traffic around the Eastern Bypass. The overall planning approval is for 1.45 million square feet, a massive scheme, that will take approximately ten years to complete.

The closure of the Rover Assembly Plant included much of the original Morris site. Its demise was a necessary step in the continuing development of Cowley.

Perhaps Cowley's best known landmark, the twin chimneys of Morris Motors, during demolition of that part of the Rover site during the spring of 1994.